WITHDRAWN

3 1526 05528581 8

WITHDRAWN

CELEBRATING
PRESIDENTS' DAY

BY TRUDI STRAIN TRUEIT · ILLUSTRATED BY MICHELLE DORENKAMP

The Child's World®
childsworld.com

Published by The Child's World®
1980 Lookout Drive • Mankato, MN 56003-1705
800-599-READ • www.childsworld.com

Copyright © 2022 by The Child's World®
All rights reserved. No part of this book may be
reproduced or utilized in any form or by any means
without written permission from the publisher.

ISBN 9781503853973 (Reinforced Library Binding)
ISBN 9781503854741 (Portable Document Format)
ISBN 9781503855120 (Online Multi-user eBook)
LCCN: 2021930090

Printed in the United States of America

ABOUT THE AUTHOR

Trudi Strain Trueit is a former television news reporter and anchor. She has written dozens of books for children. She lives in Everett, WA with her husband, Bill, a teacher.

ABOUT THE ILLUSTRATOR

Michelle Dorenkamp has illustrated more than 50 children's books for various publishers around the world. She lives in St. Louis, Missouri, and enjoys spending free time with her family.

CONTENTS

CHAPTER 1
Pride and Presidents

People crowd the sidewalks of Old Town Alexandria, Virginia. A marching band plays "Yankee Doodle." Here comes a red, white, and blue float. You're just in time for the Presidents' Day parade!

Presidents' Day falls on the third Monday in February. The holiday honors the presidents of the United States, especially George Washington (1732-1799) and Abraham Lincoln (1809-1865). Both of these leaders were born in February.

So wave an American flag and join the celebration!

The American President resembles the commander of a ship at sea. He must have a helm to grasp, a course to steer, a port to seek.
—Henry Adams (1838-1918), grandson and great-grandson of U.S. presidents John Quincy Adams and John Adams

Join the parade for Presidents' Day!

5

CHAPTER 2

Never Give Up!

George Washington was born on February 22, 1732, in Virginia **Colony**. As a boy, George dreamed of being a soldier. When he was 21 years old, George joined the Virginia **militia**.

In 1759, George married Martha Custis. They settled on George's Virginia farm called Mount Vernon. Their quiet life didn't last long.

Did you know the story about young George Washington chopping down a cherry tree isn't true? It was made up by a writer.

George and Martha Washington were farmers in the colonies.

Celebrating General Washington's birthday cheered up the troops.

The colonies were tired of obeying Great Britain. The colonists wanted to be free to rule themselves. In 1775, British and American soldiers started shooting at each other. The Revolutionary War (1775-1783) had begun!

George Washington led the colonial forces into battle. His small Continental Army was no match for the mighty British. Yet, Washington did not give up. The winter of 1778 was very cold in Valley Forge, Pennsylvania. The Continental Army didn't have enough food or supplies. On February 22nd, the troops celebrated General Washington's birthday. (He was 46.) They played music and sang. It lifted everyone's spirits.

In time, Washington's patience and clever battle plans paid off. The colonies won the war!

"Liberty, when it begins to take root, is a plant of rapid growth."
—George Washington

CHAPTER 3

Father of His Country

At last, the United States was **independent**! The new nation needed a leader. Again, people turned to Washington. Some wanted to crown him king of the country. Washington said "no." The country needed a citizen to guide it, not a king to rule it.

In 1789, Washington was chosen to be the first U.S. president. Soon, it became a **tradition** for American cities to celebrate his birthday.

I often say of George Washington that he was one of the few in the whole history of the world who was not carried away by power.
—Robert Frost (1874-1963), American poet

President Washington was a fair and kind leader.

Washington was a kind leader. At the end of his life, he expressed that he was against **slavery**. He also felt land had been wrongly taken from Native Americans. He tried to help them. After two terms (eight years), Washington went home to Virginia.

On December 14, 1799, George Washington died at Mount Vernon. The United States lost a brave hero, Founding Father, and beloved president.

"A citizen, first in war, first in peace, first in the hearts of his countryman."
—General Henry Lee (1732-1794)

CHAPTER 4

Honest Abe

Abraham Lincoln was born in a log cabin in Kentucky on February 12, 1809. Young Abe loved reading. One of his favorite books was about George Washington.

Abe was bright, funny, and honest. His good **character** got him elected to the state **legislature** in 1834. He began speaking out against slavery. In 1842, Abe married Mary Todd.

> "A house divided against itself cannot stand. I believe this government cannot endure permanently half slave and half free."
> —*Abraham Lincoln, 1858 campaign speech*

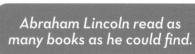

Abraham Lincoln read as many books as he could find.

Abraham Lincoln was the tallest U.S. President. He was six feet, four inches tall—about one inch taller than George Washington!

The Civil War was the bloodiest war in U.S. history.

In 1860, Lincoln became the sixteenth president of the United States. By now, the issue of slavery was splitting the nation. The South wanted to withdraw from the United States to form its own country. Lincoln was determined not to let that happen. This led to the Civil War (1861–1865). In 1863, Lincoln freed the enslaved people. But it took two more years for the North to win the war.

Lincoln was elected to a second term. On April 14, 1865, he was shot by John Wilkes Booth. Booth supported the South. He was angry about the war. Lincoln died the next morning.

Today, Lincoln is remembered as a strong president. He kept the United States together during one of its hardest times.

The U.S. Civil War lasted from 1861 to 1865. For four long years, the war divided the nation. The northern states and the southern states fought each other over the issue of slavery. The war divided families and friends. Thousands of people died. If the North hadn't won the war, the South could have become a separate country and slavery could have continued there.

CHAPTER 5

A Nation Celebrates

In 1885, U.S. President Chester Arthur declared Washington's birthday a national holiday. By now, some states were observing Abraham Lincoln's birthday, too (though it was never made a U.S. holiday).

In 1968, the U.S. **Congress** moved Washington's birthday celebration to the third Monday in February. It became more commonly known as Presidents' Day, a holiday to honor all presidents. Government offices, banks, and schools close on Presidents' Day. People fly U.S. flags. There are parades, concerts, plays, and fireworks shows. Some people lay wreaths at the Washington Monument and the Lincoln Memorial in Washington, D.C. Thousands of people show up to pay their respects at Mount Vernon!

Mount Rushmore in South Dakota is one of the most famous memorials to U.S. presidents. The heads of George Washington, Thomas Jefferson, Abraham Lincoln, and Theodore Roosevelt are carved into a granite cliff. Each face is 60 feet tall!

Many U.S. monuments and memorials honor former presidents.

It is also tradition for a senator to read George Washington's 1796 farewell address to Congress. The Father of His Country gave the nation and its people some wise advice. "Observe good faith and justice toward all nations; cultivate peace and harmony with all."

PRESIDENTS' FACES ON U.S. MONEY

Washington is on the quarter and the one dollar bill.

Lincoln is on the penny and the five dollar bill.

Thomas Jefferson is on the nickel.

Franklin Roosevelt is on the dime.

Andrew Jackson is on the twenty dollar bill.

CHAPTER 6
Hail to the Chief

Do you ever wonder what the president does? He or she works with Congress to create laws. The president meets with world leaders to keep peace. The president commands the military in times of war.

The United States has had more than forty presidents. Each one has been different. Thomas Jefferson was born into a rich family. Abraham Lincoln was very poor. Before taking the Oath of Office, Harry Truman ran a clothing store. Jimmy Carter owned a peanut farm. Ronald Reagan was a movie actor.

That is a wonderful thing about the United States. Any citizen who was born in the country can be president.

PRESIDENTIAL OATH OF OFFICE

"I do solemnly swear that I will faithfully execute the office of President of the United States, and will to the best of my ability, preserve, protect, and defend the Constitution of the United States."

Before becoming president, Jimmy Carter grew peanuts!

There are advantages to being elected President. The day after I was elected, I had my high school grades classified Top Secret.
—Ronald Reagan (1911–2004), 40th U.S. President

CHAPTER 7

Poetry Corner

A NATION'S STRENGTH

What makes a nation's pillars high
And its foundations strong?
What makes it mighty to defy
The foes that round it throng?

Brave men who work while others sleep,
Who dare while others fly . . .
They build a nation's pillars deep
And lift them to the sky.

—*Ralph Waldo Emerson (1803–1882),*
American poet

The ultimate rulers of our democracy are not a President and senators and congressmen and government officials, but the voters of this country.
—*Franklin D. Roosevelt (1882–1945),*
32nd U.S. President

PRAISE FOR A NATION

My country owes me nothing.
It gave me, as it gives to every boy and girl, a chance.
It gave me schooling, independence of action, opportunity for service and honor.
In no other land could a boy from a country village, without inheritance or influential friends, look forward with unbounded hope.

—Herbert Hoover (1874–1964),
31st U.S. President

CHAPTER 8

Songs of Presidents' Day

HAIL TO THE CHIEF

Hail to the Chief we have chosen for the nation, hail to the Chief! We salute him, one and all. Hail to the Chief, as we pledge co-operation, in proud fulfillment of a great, noble call. Yours is the aim to make this grand country grander, this you will do; that's our strong, firm belief. Hail to the one we selected as commander, hail to the President! Hail to the Chief!

—*traditional lyrics*

Any time the president attends an important event, the song "Hail to the Chief" is played in his or her honor. This tradition began in the early 1800s. The song is also played at a president's funeral.

YANKEE DOODLE DANDY

Father and I went down to camp
Along with Captain Gooding,
And there we saw the men and boys
As thick as hasty pudding.

Chorus:
Yankee doodle, keep it up
Yankee doodle dandy
Mind the music and the step
And with the girls be handy.

There was Captain Washington
Upon a slapping stallion
A-giving orders to his men,
I guess there was a million.

—*traditional lyrics*

MY COUNTRY 'TIS OF THEE

My country 'tis of thee, sweet land of liberty, of thee I sing;
Land where my fathers died, land of the pilgrims' pride,
from every mountain side let freedom ring.

My native country, thee, land of the noble free, thy name I love;
I love thy rocks and rills, thy woods and templed hills;
My heart with rapture thrills like that above.

—words by Samuel Francis Smith (1808-1895),
 minister

Let every nation know, whether it wishes us well or ill, that we shall pay any price, bear any burden, meet any hardship, support any friend, oppose any foe to assure the survival and the success of liberty.
– John F. Kennedy (1917-1963), 35th U.S. President

JOINING IN THE SPIRIT OF PRESIDENTS' DAY

* Imagine that you are the president of the United States! Make a list of some things you would work to accomplish. What would you change? How would you do it?

* Who is your favorite president and why? Write a poem or song in his honor.

* Ask a parent or grandparent about a president they remember from their childhood. What was America like when they were young? What challenges did the nation have to overcome?

* Write a thank-you letter to the president of the United States. Send it to:
    The White House
    1600 Pennsylvania Avenue NW
    Washington, DC 20500

* Go to a Presidents' Day parade, concert, or play and have fun!

MAKING A CHERRY PIE

What you need:
1 box of pre-made refrigerated pie crust
   (comes with two crusts)
2 cans of cherry pie filling

Directions
1. Preheat the oven to 400 degrees Fahrenheit.*
2. Roll out one of the pre-made crusts and place it into the bottom of a 9-inch pie plate.
3. Pour both cans of cherry pie filling into the pie crust. Even out the filling with a spoon.
4. Place the second pie crust on top of the pie.
5. Seal the edges of the two crusts together. Going around the outside of the pie plate, press a fork into the edge of the dough (an adult can help you with this).
6. With a knife, cut a small cross into the center of the pie to release steam during baking.
7. Place the pie on a cookie sheet. Bake for 40 to 45 minutes until the crust is golden brown and the filling is bubbling.
8. After baking, let the pie cool before serving.
9. Serve your cherry pie alone or à la mode (that means with a scoop of your favorite ice cream!).

*Have an adult help you operate the oven.

LOG CABIN CRAFTS

What you need:

A half-pint milk carton, washed thoroughly
Creamy peanut butter
Pretzels
Graham crackers
Wheat crackers
Cereal squares
Scissors

Directions

1. Spread the outside of the milk carton with creamy peanut butter.

2. The pretzels will be the logs on the walls of the house. Using the scissors, cut the pretzel sticks the same length as the width of the cabin.

3. Lay the sticks side by side on the peanut butter.

4. Using the cereal squares, add windows and a door.

5. Using the crackers, make the roof.

Now you have a fun log cabin craft in honor of Abraham Lincoln!

GLOSSARY

character (KAYR-ek-tur)—the quality of an individual's personality or reputation

colony (KAHL-uh-nee)—a group of people from one country who settle in another country

Congress (KONG-ress)—the national legislature of the U.S., made up of the House and Senate; the elected people who make U.S. laws

independent (in-duh-PEN-dent)—free; not under the control of others

legislature (LEJ-ih-slay-chur)—an elected group of lawmakers

militia (muh-LISH-uh)—citizens trained to fight as soldiers in an emergency

slavery (SLAY-vuh-ree)—a system where people are forced to work for others

tradition (truh-DISH-un)—a long-held custom or something people do every year

LEARN MORE

BOOKS

Barber, James. *DK Eyewitness Books: Presidents.* New York, NY: DK, 2017.

deRubertis, Barbara. *Let's Celebrate Presidents' Day.* New York, NY: Lerner Publishing Group, 2014.

DuMont, Brianna. *Weird But True Know-It-All: U.S. Presidents.* Washington, DC: National Geographic, 2017.

Homzie, Hillary. *Ellie May on Presidents' Day.* Watertown, MA: Charlesbridge, 2018.

Lewison, Wendy Cheyette. *P Is for President.* New York, NY: Grosset & Dunlap, 2016.

Rockwell Anne F. *Presidents' Day.* New York, NY: Harpercollins Childrens Books, 2010.

WEBSITES

Visit our website for links about Presidents' Day and other holidays:
childsworld.com/links

Note to Parents, Teachers, and Librarians: We routinely verify our Web links to make sure they are safe and active sites. So encourage your readers to check them out!

INDEX